Financial Interdependence and Variability in Exchange Rates

RALPH C. BRYANT

Financial Interdependence and Variability in Exchange Rates

A Staff Paper

THE BROOKINGS INSTITUTION
Washington, D.C.

1775 Massachusetts Avenue, N.W., Washington, D.C. 20036

Library of Congress Cataloging in Publication Data:

Bryant, Ralph C. 1938–

Financial Interdependence and Variability in Exchange Rates.

Includes bibliographical references.

1. Foreign exchange. 2. Foreign exchange administration. I. Brookings Institution, Washington, D.C.
II. Title.

HG3852.B79 332.4′56 80-24883

ISBN 0-8157-1127-1 (pbk.)

2 3 4 5 6 7 8 9

THE BROOKINGS INSTITUTION is an independent organization devoted to nonpartisan research, education, and publication in economics, government, foreign policy, and the social sciences generally. Its principal purposes are to aid in the development of sound public policies and to promote public understanding of issues of national importance.

The Institution was founded on December 8, 1927, to merge the activities of the Institute for Government Research, founded in 1916, the Institute of Economics, founded in 1922, and the Robert Brookings Graduate School of Economics and Government, founded in 1924.

The Board of Trustees is responsible for the general administration of the Institution, while the immediate direction of the policies, program, and staff is vested in the President, assisted by an advisory committee of the officers and staff. The by-laws of the Institution state: "It is the function of the Trustees to make possible the conduct of scientific research, and publication, under the most favorable conditions, and to safeguard the independence of the research staff in the pursuit of their studies and in the publication of the results of such studies. It is not a part of their function to determine, control, or influence the conduct of particular investigations or the conclusions reached."

The President bears final responsibility for the decision to publish a manuscript as a Brookings book. In reaching his judgment on the competence, accuracy, and objectivity of each study, the President is advised by the director of the appropriate research program and weighs the views of a panel of expert outside readers who report to him in confidence on the quality of the work. Publication of a work signifies that it is deemed a competent treatment worthy of public consideration but does not imply endorsement of conclusions or recommendations.

The Institution maintains its position of neutrality on issues of public policy in order to safeguard the intellectual freedom of the staff. Hence interpretations or conclusions in Brookings publications should be understood to be solely those of the authors and should not be attributed to the Institution, to its trustees, officers, or other staff members, or to the organizations that support its research.

Foreword

THE WORLD of international finance was in fairly continuous turmoil from the mid-1960s to 1973. A chief consequence of the turmoil was a progressive crumbling, and finally a formal dismantling, of the Bretton-Woods adjustable-peg system governing currency exchange rates. Since the abandonment of the Bretton-Woods constraints on exchange-rate movements (de facto in March 1973 and de jure in 1978 with the adoption of the revised Articles of Agreement of the International Monetary Fund), individual nations have been free to permit as much or as little variability in the external values of their currencies as they wish.

The new scope for national discretion in external monetary policy resulted in substantial variations in exchange rates, in some cases by amounts even larger than the par-value changes of 1971–73. Those variations have been the dominant focus of attention in international financial discussions in recent years. Indeed, rather than fading away after the demise of the Bretton-Woods arrangements, the long-standing debate about fixed versus flexible exchange rates has acquired a new lease on life.

That controversy is the starting point for this staff paper by Ralph C. Bryant. He shows, however, that much of the traditional debate is concerned with an artificial choice about exchange rates that national governments do not have to make and probably should not make. Policymakers and economists, he argues, need to develop a deeper understanding of exchange-rate variability under conditions of financial interdependence before they can make sound judgments about the appropriate conduct of national exchange-rate policy. The analytical framework outlined here represents a first step toward such understanding.

This paper is an offshoot of the author's treatise on the theory of economic policy, *Money and Monetary Policy in Interdependent Nations,* also published by Brookings. The arguments summarized here are developed in greater detail in that book. The book also provides an integrated analysis of exchange-rate variability and "domestic" monetary policy, showing that the principles and procedures applied to the one are equally relevant for the other.

The first version of this paper was prepared for a colloquium, "Europe and the Dollar in the World-Wide Disequilibrium," that was sponsored by the Société Universitaire Européenne de Recherches Financières (SUERF) and held in Basle, Switzerland in May 1979; it will be published with the other proceedings of the SUERF colloquium by Sijthoff & Noordhoff International Publishers in the Netherlands. The author is grateful to SUERF for providing an opportunity to present his views on exchange-rate variability and for concurring in the publication of this revision of his paper by Brookings.

The author is a senior fellow in the Brookings Economic Studies program. Before joining Brookings, he served on the staff of the Board of Governors of the Federal Reserve System as Director of the Division of International Finance and Associate Economist of the Federal Open Market Committee.

The author is indebted to his Brookings colleagues Lawrence B. Krause, Robert Z. Lawrence, Walter S. Salant, and Robert Solomon and to Gottfried Haberler for helpful comments on drafts of this essay. He is also indebted to David S. Bates and Stephen L. Smith for research assistance and to Charlotte Kaiser for typing the manuscript.

This paper and the larger project of which it is a part have received support from a Rockefeller Foundation grant.

The views expressed here are those of the author and should not be attributed to the Rockefeller Foundation or to the officers, trustees, or other staff members of the Brookings Institution.

BRUCE K. MAC LAURY
President

Washington, D.C.
June 1980

Financial Interdependence and Variability in Exchange Rates

EXCHANGE RATES between major currencies varied by large amounts in the 1970s, both before and after the breakdown in March 1973 of the Bretton Woods adjustable-peg regime. Many analysts of international finance regard this variability as undesirable. For example, some assert that variability in exchange rates has caused "instability of the international monetary system." But others ardently champion exchange-rate variability. They view the abandonment of the Bretton Woods regime as an unambiguous improvement in the international monetary system and regard efforts to prevent exchange-rate variability as a retrograde step.

My purpose here is to put such disagreements about exchange-rate variability into better perspective by making some analytical observations about national macroeconomic developments under conditions of financial interdependence. I concentrate on the implications for economic interrelations between Europe and North America, but I do not espouse an "American view." On the contrary, my intent is to present an impartial analysis of exchange-rate variability as it affects the interests of nations on both sides of the Atlantic—indeed, of all nations constituting the interdependent global economy.

My analysis provides a basis for evaluating four widely held views about exchange rates. The first of these—most often encountered in Europe and Japan, but also popular elsewhere, even in North America—may be labeled the *minimum-variance* position. Those holding this view emphasize the uncertainty and disruption that may be associated with fluctuations in exchange rates and argue that governments should act to "maintain as much exchange-rate stability as possible."[1] Proponents of the European Monetary System who identify the creation of a "zone of monetary stability" as the primary objective of those exchange-rate arrangements appear to advocate the minimum-variance position (at least for fluctuations of exchange rates between EEC currencies).

A second view, the *untrammeled-market* position, holds that every nation should pursue appropriate domestic macroeconomic policies and then permit currency values to be freely determined in the exchange market without any intervention by central banks and governments. While held most vigorously by some economists and government officials in North America, this position too is often encountered elsewhere.

A third view, labeled here the *insulation* position, holds that "flexible exchange rates are a means of combining interdependence among countries through trade with a maximum of internal monetary independence" and that "they are a means of permitting each country to seek for monetary stability according to its own lights, without either imposing its mistakes on its neighbors or having their mistakes imposed on it."[2] A sweeping version of this view asserts that exchange-rate flexibility bottles up policy actions and nonpolicy disturbances within the nation where they originate, thereby completely insulating other nations from their consequences. A more cautious version, as the preceding quotation implies, asserts only that flexible rates insulate nations from each other's "monetary" disturbances. This view is a first cousin to the untrammeled-market position. If exchange-rate variability is believed to insulate national economies, it may also seem to promise an unshackling of domestic macroeconomic policies from international constraints, freeing those policies to concentrate on internal economic developments.

A fourth view, here termed the *international monetary reform* position, is more eclectic about the appropriate manner and degree of exchange-rate variability among major currencies. According to this view, however, it is important for nations to agree on some compromise set of provisions governing exchange rates and external reserve positions. Current world monetary arrangements are described as anarchic. Despite the failure of the reform effort of the Committee of 20 in 1972–74,

1. See Tom de Vries, "The Inconstant Dollar," *Foreign Policy*, no. 32 (Fall 1978), pp. 161–62. De Vries designates the minimum-variance position and the untrammeled-market position (summarized in the following text) as "European" and "North American" views, respectively.

2. Milton Friedman, "The Case for Flexible Exchange Rates," *Essays in Positive Economics* (University of Chicago Press, 1953), p. 200.

proponents of this view argue, there is an urgent need to develop a new "supranational rule of law" for the international monetary system.

Each of these four views, I believe, is seriously misleading if not flatly wrong. And each can lead to inappropriate judgments about the conduct of national macroeconomic policies and about the scope for international monetary cooperation.

The Degree of Exchange-Rate Variability in the 1970s

Discussions of fluctuations in exchange rates often focus merely on spot exchange rates with the U.S. dollar. That focus can yield a misleading impression of the effective degree of variability. As a prelude to the analysis that follows, therefore, a brief reminder of the complexity of the empirical experience of the 1970s is instructive.

Table 1 presents data for the percentage changes in external value of seven major currencies for various subperiods of the 1970s. Changes are shown for two measures of a nation's weighted-average exchange rate as well as for the spot exchange rate of its currency with the U.S. dollar. One of the weighted-average measures is the series calculated by the staff of the Federal Reserve Board; it weights individual spot exchange rates with the shares of countries in the *total* trade of the Group of Ten countries plus Switzerland ("multilateral" trade weights).[3] The other weighted-average measure shown in table 1, the series published by Morgan Guaranty Trust Company, assigns weights to individual foreign currencies according to the shares of countries in the trade of the nation for which the average is calculated ("bilateral" trade weights).[4] The time series underlying table 1 are also plotted in the set of seven charts that constitute the appendix to this paper.

The subperiods shown in table 1 are not of equal length. Their differing durations have been selected to highlight some of the decade's major swings in exchange rates. The peak and trough months that define the

3. See Peter Hooper and John Morton, "Summary Measures of the Dollar's Foreign Exchange Value," *Federal Reserve Bulletin* (October 1978), pp. 783–89. The series for the United States and other nations are charted weekly in "Selected Interest and Exchange Rates," Release H.13 (Federal Reserve System, 1970–79).

4. See Morgan Guaranty Trust Company of New York, "Effective Exchange Rates: Nominal and Real," *World Financial Markets* (May 1978), and "Effective Exchange Rates Compared," *World Financial Markets* (April 1979).

Table 1. *Alternative Measures of Variat*

			Pe
Nation and type of exchange-rate measure	*June 1970 to March 1973*	*March 1973 to July 1973*	*July 197 to Janua 197*
Germany			
Weighted average exchange rate, bilateral trade weights[a]	+8.7	+11.7	−4
Weighted average exchange rate, multilateral trade weights[b]	+13.5	+16.4	−8
Spot exchange rate with U.S. dollar	+29.1	+20.5	−17
France			
Weighted average exchange rate, bilateral trade weights[a]	+2.3	+1.6	−7
Weighted average exchange rate, multilateral trade weights[b]	+6.1	+5.2	−10
Spot exchange rate with U.S. dollar	+22.5	+11.1	−19
Italy			
Weighted average exchange rate, bilateral trade weights[a]	−8.8	−12.5	+4
Weighted average exchange rate, multilateral trade weights[b]	−5.0	−8.5	+0
Spot exchange rate with U.S. dollar	+10.7	−2.3	−10
United Kingdom			
Weighted average exchange rate, bilateral trade weights[a]	−13.6	−5.5	−0
Weighted average exchange rate, multilateral trade weights[b]	−12.3	−3.6	−2
Spot exchange rate with U.S. dollar	+3.1	+2.6	−12
Japan			
Weighted average exchange rate, bilateral trade weights[a]	+26.0	−4.6	−6
Weighted average exchange rate, multilateral trade weights[b]	+20.4	−7.3	−0
Spot exchange rate with U.S. dollar	+37.1	−1.0	−11
Canada			
Weighted average exchange rate, bilateral trade weights[a]	+1.3	−1.1	+3
Weighted average exchange rate, multilateral trade weights[b]	−11.0	−6.5	+14
Spot exchange rate with U.S. dollar	+4.2	−0.3	+0
United States			
Weighted average exchange rate, bilateral trade weights[a]	−14.1	−3.3	+8
Weighted average exchange rate, multilateral trade weights[b]	−17.3	−7.3	+15
Spot exchange rate with German mark	−22.5	−17.0	+20
Spot exchange rate with Japanese yen	−27.1	+1.0	+12

a. Source: Morgan Guaranty Trust Company.
b. Source: Federal Reserve Board staff.
c. Underlying spot exchange rates and weighted indexes are monthly averages of daily rates.

change Rates, Selected Periods, 1970–80

iation (+) or depreciation (−) of national currency[c]

January 1974 to March 1975	*March 1975 to September 1977*	*September 1977 to October 1978*	*October 1978 to May 1979*	*May 1979 to January 1980*	*January 1980 to April 1980*	*June 1970 to January 1980*
+4.4	+12.7	+6.8	+0.4	+3.7	−2.2	+52.1
+11.4	+9.5	+11.1	+0.1	+7.2	−4.1	+75.9
+21.4	−0.2	+26.5	−3.7	+10.6	−8.1	+110.6
+3.8	−5.4	−2.3	−1.1	+1.9	−0.8	−6.2
+8.8	−8.6	+1.1	−1.0	+5.1	−2.7	+4.5
+19.6	−14.7	+17.0	−4.5	+9.1	−7.1	+36.7
−12.5	−22.8	−9.6	−1.1	−1.8	−1.8	−50.4
−7.9	−24.2	−6.6	−1.0	+1.5	−3.6	−42.8
+2.7	−28.6	+8.8	−4.7	+5.8	−8.1	−21.8
−5.2	−22.4	−1.8	+6.9	+4.3	+3.4	−34.7
−2.1	−24.0	−0.7	+7.3	+5.9	+2.8	−30.6
+8.7	−27.9	+15.2	+2.6	+10.0	−2.4	−5.6
−1.8	+14.9	+35.9	−14.0	−11.5	−2.7	+31.3
−7.4	+18.9	+28.9	−14.1	−13.4	−0.1	+16.8
+3.5	+7.9	+45.3	−15.9	−8.2	−4.9	+50.9
−2.6	−4.9	−12.3	+3.3	−1.3	−1.0	−14.7
−11.4	+0.9	−23.2	+6.8	−5.2	+3.4	−34.1
−0.9	−6.8	−9.3	+2.4	−0.7	−1.9	−10.8
−5.9	+8.0	−10.3	+3.8	−1.1	+4.9	−15.9
−12.3	+10.5	−17.1	+5.0	−5.3	+6.5	−29.3
−17.6	+0.2	−21.0	+3.9	−9.6	+8.8	−52.5
−3.4	−7.3	−31.2	+19.0	+8.9	+5.2	−33.7

subperiods correspond to the months in which the U.S. dollar reached interim highs or lows; but those months also correspond roughly to the trough and peak months for several of the other currencies.[5]

A weighted-average measure is typically a much better gauge of "the" exchange rate for a nation's currency than its spot rate with a single foreign currency—even when that currency is as important as the U.S. dollar.[6] As table 1 and the appendix charts show, the weighted-average rates vary by significantly smaller amounts for most nations over most time intervals. The episode of dollar depreciation from September 1977 to October 1978 is a striking but not atypical example. The German mark and the Japanese yen appreciated bilaterally against the dollar by some 27 percent and 45 percent, respectively, but their corresponding appreciations against an average of major currencies were considerably less—only some 7–11 percent in the case of the mark. During the same period, the French franc and sterling appreciated sharply against the dollar but remained essentially unchanged on an average basis; the Italian lira strengthened against the dollar by 9 percent but *depreciated* against all currencies collectively by some 7–10 percent. Italy's experience with the lira in 1977–78 is not an isolated case. Table 1 contains a number of additional examples, for Italy and for the United Kingdom and Japan, of movements of the weighted-average exchange rate and the spot dollar rate in *opposite* directions.

The apparent degree of variability in exchange rates is also sensitive to the choice of the weighted-average measure. As table 1 and the appendix charts show, for some nations an index calculated with bilateral trade weights exhibits significantly less variability than an index based on multilateral trade weights. This generalization has been especially applicable in the 1970s to the United States, but has also been characteristic of Germany and France. For other nations—for example, Italy, Japan, and Canada—an index with bilateral trade weights has a greater variance. Indeed, because the great bulk of Canada's trade is conducted with the United States, an index for Canada using bilateral trade weights moves similarly to the spot exchange rate with the U.S. dollar.

5. For some analytical purposes, for example appraising trends in the prices of tradable goods or trends in inflation-adjusted (so-called real) exchange rates, this selection of subperiods is patently inappropriate.

6. This statement is true despite the fact that exchange-market transactions always involve currency pairs, not currency averages.

Many alternative measures of weighted-average exchange rates may be calculated. Each has its advantages and limitations. No single average is preferable for all analytical purposes.[7]

While table 1 and the appendix charts caution against discussing currency values solely in terms of dollar exchange rates, they also show that each of the major nations has experienced sizable fluctuations even on a weighted-average basis. To focus on one example: the Federal Reserve index of the dollar's average value in relation to other major currencies between March 1973 and April 1980 went down by 7 percent, up by 15½ percent, down by 12 percent, up by 10½ percent, down by 17 percent, up by 5 percent, down by 5 percent, and then up by 6½ percent (measured by peak and trough months as in table 1). The swings for all the currencies would be still larger if measured from peaks and troughs for individual days instead of monthly averages.

Consequences of Macroeconomic Disturbances under Alternative Assumptions about Exchange-Rate Variability

No matter how variability is measured, an analytical framework is a prerequisite for evaluation of alternative views about exchange-rate variability. I assume for this section of the paper a simplified framework and indicate in abbreviated form the type of conclusions it can yield.[8]

Imagine a world composed of only two nations, Europa and America, whose currency units are the ecu and the dollar and whose gross national products and populations are roughly comparable in size. Each nation

7. An average using bilateral trade weights emphasizes the particular geographical characteristics of a nation's trade but does not allow for the effects of trade competition in third markets. An average based on multilateral trade weights allows for third-market competition but may overstate its importance. Neither measure gives weight to international financial transactions. For further discussion see Rudolf R. Rhomberg, "Indices of Effective Exchange Rates," *IMF Staff Papers,* vol. 23 (March 1976), pp. 88–112; Hooper and Morton, "Summary Measures"; and Morgan Guaranty Trust Company, "Effective Exchange Rates" and "Effective Exchange Rates Compared." Similar issues arise when considering alternative techniques for determining the national currency valuation of "supranational" assets such as special drawing rights (SDRs); see, for example, J. J. Polak, "The SDR as a Basket of Currencies," *IMF Staff Papers,* vol. 26 (December 1979), pp. 627–53.

8. The discussion that follows is based on the analysis in chapters 20–22 of my book, *Money and Monetary Policy in Interdependent Nations* (Brookings Institution, 1980).

imports from and exports to the other on a substantial scale because economic units in both nations are accustomed to consuming goods produced abroad as well as those produced at home. Banks and some nonbank economic units in each nation have assets and liabilities vis-à-vis foreign residents, including assets and liabilities denominated in the other nation's currency. Regulatory impediments shut off a few channels of capital flow between the two nations, but the impediments are not comprehensive and do not prevent substantial international shifts among assets in response to changes in expectations of the exchange rate, interest rates, and asset prices.

The two national economies are thus inseparable parts of an interdependent world economy. Most residents of each nation, however, are less familiar with or do not prefer imported goods; at prevailing relative prices, they allocate the bulk of their expenditures to goods produced at home. Similarly, many residents of each nation are not familiar with or prefer not to take advantage of opportunities for investment and borrowing in foreign financial markets or in the foreign currency unit.

These relations between the economies of Europa and America may be described as *partial* or *intermediate* interdependence. Policy actions or nonpolicy disturbances originating in one nation inevitably have more than trivial effects in the other nation. Yet the effects abroad are typically weaker than they are in the originating nation.

While economically interdependent, Europa and America are politically independent. The policymakers of each nation have national objectives—for example, policymakers in Europa are deeply concerned with employment and the price level in Europa but may attach little if any welfare value per se to employment and the price level in America—and are free to adjust the instruments of national macroeconomic policy in whatever manner they think best.

Let the "international monetary system" in this two-nation world be akin to that defined in the current Articles of Agreement of the International Monetary Fund. In particular, suppose that there are no binding supranational constraints on movements of exchange rates and external reserve assets.

Finally, assume some benchmark outcome for the evolution of the world economy as a whole, one that is regarded as attainable and desirable by policymakers in both Europa and America. The characteristics of this benchmark outcome—for example, the specific time paths for each nation of such target variables as real output, the price level, and employment, together with the settings on macroeconomic policy instruments that are consistent with attainment or maintenance of those desired targets—are not essential for the analysis and can therefore remain unspecified. The benchmark outcome serves here solely as a standard of comparison by which alternative, less desirable outcomes can be judged.

In each of the four subsections that follow, I postulate that a macroeconomic disturbance occurs which makes the benchmark outcome unattainable with the original settings of the two nations' policy instruments. The consequences of the disturbance for the two national economies—measured by the differences in variables from their values in the benchmark case—depend on, among other things, whether the dollar-ecu exchange rate is held fixed or allowed to vary. The brief summaries of the consequences presented in what follows focus on the contrasts between the fixed-rate and variable-rate outcomes.

The purpose of the analysis here is to draw inferences about appropriate policies for a single nation. Arbitrarily, the discussion adopts the perspective of policymakers in Europa.[9]

Recession in America. As a first illustration, consider a sharp decline in economic activity in America caused by an unexpected increase in the saving rate of American consumers and an unexpected slump in American business investment (all relative to the benchmark case). The decline in the nominal value of aggregate activity in America results chiefly from a fall in real output; but the American rate of inflation also falls somewhat.

The unexpected decline in consumption and investment and the onset of the resulting recession put *incipient* pressures on financial variables in America and Europa. The incipient pressures include tendencies for market interest rates in America to fall, for the ecu to depreciate (the dollar to appreciate), and for market interest rates in Europa to fall. *Actual* adjustments in financial variables depend on how domestic mone-

9. The analytical generalizations that follow are strongly influenced by the financial as well as the real-sector interdependence of the two economies. The network of asset and liability relations assumed to link Europa and America can give rise to international capital flows whenever financial variables such as interest rates, the exchange rate, and asset supplies are altered. In its treatment of financial interdependence, my analysis incorporates the recent progress reflected in the literatures on the portfolio-balance approach to capital flows and the asset-market approach to exchange-rate determination. For an excellent survey of the latter, see Peter Isard, *The Process of Exchange-Rate Determination: A Survey of Important Models and Major Issues,* Princeton Study in International Finance No. 42 (Princeton University Press, May 1978).

tary policy is implemented in the two nations and on the extent of exchange-market interventions, if any.[10]

If sufficient central-bank purchases of ecus against dollars are carried out in the exchange market to resist the tendency of the ecu to depreciate, the external reserve position of Europa will decline (the external reserve position of America will increase). If the central bank in Europa keeps interest rates in Europa from falling because it uses a short-term interest rate as the primary instrument of domestic monetary policy and keeps that rate unchanged, "central-bank money" (the monetary base) in Europa will decrease. Europan exports to America will decline; Europan real output will fall; and some downward pressure will be exerted on the Europan price level. The American recession will be transmitted to Europa to the greatest possible extent when the dollar-ecu exchange rate remains fixed and no change occurs in the interest-rate instrument of Europan domestic monetary policy.[11]

If, on the other hand, there is no central-bank intervention in the exchange market and the ecu thus depreciates, Europa will be less adversely affected by the recession in America. Output and prices in Europa are still likely to be lower than in the benchmark case, but higher than they would be if the exchange rate were held unchanged. Conceivably, the ecu could depreciate enough and the effects of the depreciation on goods markets in Europa could be strong enough to produce an *expansion* of Europan output and *upward* pressure on the Europan price level.[12]

10. From the perspective of Europan policymakers analyzing the influences on Europa, the specific causes of the American recession importantly influence the quantitative consequences for Europan variables. Conceivably, those causes may even determine the direction of the incipient pressures on the exchange rate and the qualitative consequences for Europa. The analysis summarized in the text concludes that an autonomous drop in private-sector expenditures in America, in the medium run if not also in the short run, puts pressure on the dollar to *appreciate*. Some theoretical analysis, however, produces the opposite result that an autonomous decline in the private expenditures of a nation's residents can put pressure on the national currency to *depreciate,* at least in the short run. Less equivocal conclusions on this point require further research. This troublesome ambiguity in the direction of movement of the exchange rate does not exist if it is assumed that the American recession is caused by an excessively contractionary monetary policy; in that case, theoretical analysis unambiguously shows an appreciation of the dollar.

11. If the Europan central bank uses the quantity of central-bank money as its primary instrument of domestic monetary policy and if it keeps that quantity unchanged, interest rates in Europa will decline; the downward pressure on Europan output and prices will then be mitigated somewhat relative to the outcome in which interest rates are not permitted to fall.

12. The question of whether, pari passu with the depreciation of the ecu, output and prices in Europa are likely to fall somewhat or to increase is still a controversial,

Europan policymakers thus have a sound reason for rejecting exchange-rate "stability" in response to a sharp recession in America. Depreciation of the ecu, though not desirable in itself, is an integral part of a process helping to buffer output, employment, and the price level in Europa from the disturbance originating abroad.

A similar analysis applies to the case of an unexpected expansionary stimulus originating in America. Output and prices in Europa would be pushed upward by an American inflationary boom if the exchange rate were held unchanged. If the ecu were permitted to appreciate, however, the upward pressures would be moderated; conceivably, output and prices in Europa might even fall. Variability rather than fixity in the exchange rate would again better mitigate the adverse consequences of the foreign disturbance for Europa.

Recession in Europa. Continue to assess outcomes from the perspective of Europan policymakers. And now consider a recession that originates within Europa, caused by an unexpected decline in the consumption and investment expenditures of Europan households and firms.

The incipient pressures on financial variables in this situation include tendencies for the ecu to appreciate against the dollar (in the medium run if not also in the short run), and for market interest rates to fall in both Europa and America.[13]

If the exchange rate is prevented from changing, the external reserve position of Europa will increase. Europan output will fall, unemployment will increase, and the price level will be subjected to downward pressure. As Europan imports fall, however, some of the contractionary impetus of the recession will be transmitted to American output and prices through the current account in the balance of payments.[14]

If the exchange rate is permitted to respond to the incipient pressures stemming from the private-sector disturbance, however, less of the contractionary impetus will be transmitted to the American economy. The

unresolved issue in the theoretical literature. The small amount of existing empirical research germane to this issue has also yielded ambiguous conclusions.

13. Some theoretical models yield the conclusion that the ecu can depreciate rather than appreciate after an autonomous decline in Europan expenditures. The remarks about the direction of movement of the exchange rate in footnote 10 apply, *mutatis mutandis,* to the analysis of a recession originating in Europa.

14. The extent of the recession in Europa is most severe when the Europan central bank uses an interest rate as the main instrument of domestic monetary policy and permits market interest rates to fall, if at all, only sluggishly. If the Europan central bank keeps the quantity of central-bank money unchanged, the contraction in activity pulls down market interest rates which in turn serves to dampen the extent of the decline in output and prices.

appreciation of the ecu will work to reinforce the excess supply in Europan goods markets created by the initial disturbance. This is true for several reasons. The appreciation reduces the ecu price of imported American goods relative to the ecu price of goods produced in Europa, causing Europan residents to switch their expenditures away from Europan to American goods. Europan firms have reduced incentives to produce because of the same change in relative prices. And since the exchange-rate change alters relative prices in America (the dollar price of imported Europan goods rises relative to the dollar price of American goods), households and firms in America also switch their expenditures away from Europan to American goods.

If the objective of Europan policymakers is to minimize disruptive impacts on output, employment, and the price level in Europa, it is better to share to the greatest extent possible the adverse consequences of the internally generated recession with the American economy. Exchange-rate variability in these circumstances, therefore, because it bottles up the contractionary pressures to a greater extent within Europa, is an inferior alternative to exchange-rate "stability."[15]

A similar analysis applies to the case of a sudden expansionary stimulus originating within Europa. Fixity rather than variability in the exchange rate will force a larger proportion of the unwanted stimulus to spill over to the American economy, mitigating somewhat the inflationary consequences within Europa.

The central point to be emphasized about this second type of disturbance, of course, is that its implications for Europan policy are the opposite of those of the first type. From the selfish perspective of Europa, exchange-rate variability is undesirable when it helps to bottle up internally generated booms or recessions within Europa but desirable when it helps to buffer Europa against booms or recessions that are generated externally.

The same analysis suggests that American policymakers should prefer exchange-rate variability when a boom or recession originates in Europa but exchange-rate stability when a boom or recession originates within America. Regardless of where the booms or recessions originate, the

15. This conclusion applies to the short and medium run. Over the long run, as the tendency toward surplus (deficit) in the current account of the balance of payments of Europa (America) persists, the decreases in the external reserve position of America may be unsustainable. A change in the exchange rate may become unavoidable even in the medium run if private-sector investors develop expectations that the governments will be unable to hold the exchange rate unchanged.

national interests of the two regions have conflicting implications for exchange-rate policy!

Private-Sector Shift out of Dollar-Denominated into Ecu-Denominated Assets. As a third illustrative disturbance, suppose that private-sector investors unexpectedly decide to sell dollar-denominated assets in exchange for ecu-denominated assets, thereby reducing the desired proportion of dollar assets in their portfolios. Suppose the shift in asset preferences is a once-and-for-all and potentially even reversible change (generated, for example, by a period of political turbulence in America). For the purposes of this illustration, it is immaterial whether the shift is initiated by investors resident in America, in Europa, or in both nations. The incipient pressures on financial variables resulting from the shift include tendencies for market interest rates in America to rise, for the ecu to appreciate, and for market interest rates in Europa to fall.

If there is no central-bank intervention in the exchange market and the ecu appreciates, Europan and American residents will switch their expenditures away from goods produced in Europa in response to the change in relative prices brought about by the ecu appreciation; firms in Europa will have analogous incentives to reduce production. Thus the net result of the asset and expenditure decisions of the private sectors in both nations will be unexpected and unwanted effects on output and the price level in Europa (as always, relative to the benchmark outcome). These effects will be unambiguously contractionary if the Europan central bank keeps market interest rates in Europa from falling. If the central bank keeps the quantity of Europan central-bank money unchanged, the fall in Europan interest rates and the appreciation of the ecu will have effects on Europan output and prices that work in opposite directions; it is therefore less clear a priori that the net influence on Europan output and prices will be contractionary. The variability in the exchange rate brought about by the asset shift will generate an unwanted expansionary stimulus to output and prices in America.

If sufficient central-bank purchases of dollar assets in exchange for ecu assets are carried out to resist the tendency of the ecu to appreciate, the external reserve position of Europa will increase and that of America will decline; but there will be no unwanted effects on output and prices in either of the two nations. In effect, the two central banks will accommodate the shift in asset preferences of the world private sector at the existing financial "prices" (interest rates and the exchange rate) by means of offsetting "quantity changes" on their own balance sheets.

For this nonpersisting and possibly reversible disturbance in financial markets, Europa is better off if the exchange rate and interest rates do not adjust in response. Achievement of America's macroeconomic policy objectives is likewise unambiguously facilitated by exchange-market intervention to prevent the exchange rate from varying.

Internal Asset Shift within Europa. As a final illustration, imagine an unexpected, once-and-for-all asset shift by Europan residents reducing the demand for ecu-denominated money and correspondingly increasing the demand for ecu-denominated securities (with saving and wealth unchanged). The incipient pressures on financial variables stemming from such an unexpected decrease in the demand for ecu money include tendencies for market interest rates in Europa to fall and for the ecu to depreciate.

If the ecu is permitted to depreciate, the net outcome of the asset and expenditure decisions of the private sectors in Europa and America will be an unwanted expansionary stimulus to output and prices in Europa and, probably, unwanted downward pressure on output and the price level in America. If central-bank intervention prevents the exchange rate from varying, however, it is possible that output and prices in both nations can remain unaffected.[16]

This further example of a nonpersisting shift in private-sector asset preferences, even though the shift is an "internal" disturbance originating within Europa, thus leads to a verdict analogous to that in the preceding case. It is preferable, from the perspective of policymakers in both Europa and America, to accommodate the shifts in private asset preferences by means of quantity adjustments on the central-bank balance sheets rather than to permit changes in the exchange rate and in market interest rates.

Relevance of Analysis for Europe and North America Today. Even as a description of macroeconomic interactions in a theoretical global

16. If the exchange rate is kept unchanged and if both central banks use a market interest rate as their primary instrument of domestic monetary policy and keep market interest rates from changing, then the quantities of central-bank money, deposit money, and securities in both currencies available to be held by the world private sector will adjust to offset exactly the change in private-sector asset preferences. If the Europan central bank permits market interest rates in Europa to fall in response to the reduction in the demand for ecu money, some unwanted stimulus will be imparted to Europan output and prices (but less than will occur if interest rates are permitted to fall *and* the ecu is permitted to depreciate).

economy of two nations, the preceding analysis should be regarded as tentative. Details and qualifications have been omitted for the sake of brevity. As pointed out in my book *Money and Monetary Policy in Interdependent Nations,* further theoretical and empirical research is required on a number of aspects of the analysis as a precondition for definitive conclusions. Furthermore, the schematic analysis here abstracts from a wide range of phenomena, not least macroeconomic interactions within Europe itself, of great importance for economic interrelations among the real nations of Europe and North America.

Nonetheless, I believe that the preceding analysis provides genuine insight into the actual problems of exchange-rate variability in today's world economy. In the rest of this paper I assume that similarities between the hypothetical analysis and the real world are sufficiently strong to justify an identification of Europe with "Europa" and of the United States plus Canada with "America." Analogously, the "dollar-ecu exchange rate" is taken as a proxy for the exchange relations between the North American currencies and the linked currencies of the European Monetary System of the European Economic Community (EEC).

External Monetary Policy from a National Perspective

With the foregoing discussion as a basis for evaluation, consider now the first two views identified at the beginning of this paper. For the moment, confine the evaluation to the perspective of policymakers in European countries and assume they are concerned only with achievement of European objectives. How should they view variability in the EEC currencies against the dollar? Should they adopt the minimum-variance position and reject the untrammeled-market position, or should they make the opposite choice?

If the preceding analysis is accepted, neither of those positions is sensible. Variability of the linked European currencies against the currencies of non-European nations facilitates adjustment to some disturbances, but aggravates the adverse consequences of others. European policymakers are therefore better off with an eclectic approach.

When the EEC currencies float freely against the rest of the world, the consequences of unforeseen shifts in private asset preferences (both within Europe and between assets denominated in EEC currencies and those denominated in dollars) tend to be more adverse for European economic objectives than when the EEC currencies are kept unchanged against the dollar. For a number of unforeseen disturbances originating internally in the real (that is, nonfinancial) sectors of the European economy, exchange-rate variability with the rest of the world can likewise exacerbate the adverse effects on European output and prices, at least in the shorter run. For many other unforeseen disturbances, for example those originating abroad within the real sectors of non-European economies, the adverse effects on European economic activity tend to be greatest when exchange-rate variability with the rest of the world is prevented.

An analysis similar to that in the preceding section applies to policy "mistakes" (macroeconomic policy actions that turn out in retrospect to have been undesirable). When policy mistakes are made in North America, for example, variability of the EEC currencies against the dollar helps to mitigate the consequences of the mistakes for European economic objectives. When policy mistakes are made by European governments, on the other hand, the external monetary policy that is preferable for Europe in the shorter run is to maintain an unchanged exchange relationship of the EEC currencies to the dollar, thereby causing more of the consequences of the mistakes in domestic policy to spill over into the rest of the world.

So long as attention is myopically focused on the interests of a single nation or a single group of nations in a currency arrangement such as the European Monetary System, therefore, exchange-rate variability cannot reasonably be labeled as either good or bad. A "flexprice" external monetary policy sometimes provides better buffering for national economic objectives against disturbances, but at other times provides less buffering than a "fixprice" policy. Neither of the extreme policy rules embodied in the minimum-variance and the untrammeled-market positions can possibly be the appropriate national policy for coping with all types of disturbances.

It follows that it is inappropriate to regard either the absence or the presence of exchange-rate variability as a goal of national macroeconomic policy. The choice between fixed versus flexible exchange rates as traditionally debated in the literature of economics is an artificial choice. In the absence of binding supranational constraints such as those in the Bretton Woods version of the IMF Articles of Agreement, a national government does not have to make that choice, and should not make it. The preferable approach is to adopt discretionary procedures analogous to those taken for granted in the formulation of domestic monetary policy. Policymakers should avoid pegging either the exchange rate or the quantity of external reserves; whichever of the two is used as the instrument of external monetary policy should be discretionarily varied in response to economic developments within the nation and in the rest of the world.

Such a discretionary approach implies substantial variability over time in *both* the exchange rate and the external reserve position. This joint variability may be labeled either "managed fixing" or "managed floating" of exchange rates, or "managed pegging" or "managed variations" of external reserves. The label itself has no substantive importance; the key word, in any case, is "managed."[17]

The essence of a discretionary approach to instrument variation, for both the external and domestic instruments of national policy, is to respond differentially to different disturbances affecting the economy. For many types of disturbances, for example those known to originate in financial markets, policymakers should wish most of the adjustment in the external sector of the economy to fall on the external reserve position while the exchange rate changes little. For disturbances such as those originating in foreign markets for goods and services, it will be preferable for the exchange rate to do most of the adjusting while the external reserve position changes only slightly. The appropriateness of these responses depends little on whether the policymakers use the exchange rate or the external reserve position as their instrument.[18]

For expositional clarity, the preceding discussion summarizes the rationale for managed floating from the perspective of a single group of nations, the European Economic Community as a whole. But the analysis is general. When attention is focused myopically on the external mone-

17. The literature on domestic monetary policy contains no debate about the merits of fixed versus floating interest rates (at least not in the form characteristic of the literature on exchange-rate flexibility). That omission is a significant clue to the artificiality of the traditional debate in international economics about fluctuations in exchange rates.

18. If the exchange rate should do most of the adjusting in response to a particular disturbance, the setting for policy will have to be changed if the exchange rate is the instrument but may not need to be changed at all if the external reserve position is the instrument. The converse applies when a particular disturbance calls for most of the adjustment to fall on the external reserve position.

tary policy of individual nations, whether inside or outside Europe, analogous considerations justify the same conclusions.[19]

Can Exchange-Rate Variability Insulate National Economies?

The analytical framework summarized above undermines the conventional view of the "insulating" properties of exchange-rate variability (the third view identified at the beginning of this paper) just as it undermines the untrammeled-market position.[20] Under the conditions of intermediate interdependence, monetary-policy actions in foreign nations affect financial and real-sector variables in the home nation's economy no matter what happens to the exchange rate. Monetary-policy actions taken by the home nation's central bank are not completely bottled up at home regardless of the form and degree of exchange-rate variability. Analogous conclusions apply to the international consequences of fiscal-policy actions and of nonpolicy disturbances.

To illustrate this conclusion, revert for a moment to the analytical world economy composed of Europa and America and consider the short-run consequences in Europan financial markets of an expansionary "domestic" open-market operation by the American central bank (a purchase of dollar-denominated securities resulting in an expansion of the

19. An analytical framework of the sort outlined in this paper has great relevance for appraising the 1978–79 initiative to expand and modify the exchange links among European currencies (the so-called European snake arrangements) into the European Monetary System. If the analysis is extended to cover individual European nations as well as Europe's relations with the outside world, for example, it would rank a policy of managed floating as superior, from the perspective of each separate nation within Europe, to both the minimum-variance and the untrammeled-market positions. Similarly, it would indicate that the notion of a "zone of monetary stability" within Europe is highly problematic without a commitment by European policymakers to promptly change the parity grid of intra-European exchange rates if unavoidable divergences occur in the EEC nations' objectives and domestic macroeconomic policies. For amplification of these points, see my comments on the papers by Jacques van Ypersele and Robert Triffin in Philip H. Trezise, ed., *The European Monetary System: Its Promise and Prospects* (Brookings Institution, 1979), pp. 17–24 and 73–80.

20. The argument summarized here is developed in greater detail in chapter 23 of my *Money and Monetary Policy*.

monetary base in America). If the ecu-dollar exchange rate is held unchanged by central-bank intervention in the exchange market and if the Europan central bank holds interest rates in Europa unchanged, the external reserve position and the monetary base of Europa will increase. If the exchange rate is held unchanged and the Europan central bank holds the Europan monetary base unchanged, the external reserve position of Europa will increase and interest rates on ecu-denominated securities will rise. If the external reserve positions of both nations are held unchanged and the Europan central bank keeps Europan interest rates unchanged, the ecu will appreciate and the monetary base in Europa will be altered. If external reserve positions are unchanged and the Europan central bank keeps the Europan monetary base unchanged, the ecu will appreciate and interest rates in Europa will be altered. In no conceivable case can all key variables in the Europan financial sector remain unchanged after the monetary-policy action taken in America. Indeed, regardless of the form and degree of exchange-rate variability, intermediate interdependence between Europan and American financial markets is pervasive enough for the domestic operating procedures of the American central bank to condition the effects of Europan monetary-policy actions on the Europan economy.[21]

Now extend the analysis of this illustration to the medium run and consider the financial and real sectors of the Europan economy together. Because some key financial variables in Europa are altered no matter what happens to the exchange rate, there is no conceivable way that the prices and outputs of goods produced in Europa, the price level in Europa, and the volume of Europan employment can be completely insulated from monetary-policy actions taken in America.

More broadly, any policy action taken in America gets transmitted in one way or another to Europan output, prices, and employment—and vice versa. No analytical model of "flexible exchange rates" can be made

21. The conclusions in this paragraph may be derived from the analysis of the short-run interdependence of national financial markets in Lance Girton and Dale W. Henderson, "Financial Capital Movements and Central Bank Behavior in a Two-Country, Short-run Portfolio Balance Model," *Journal of Monetary Economics* (January 1976); and Girton and Henderson, "Central Bank Operations in Foreign and Domestic Assets Under Fixed and Flexible Exchange Rates," in *The Effects of Exchange Rate Adjustments,* edited by P. Clark, D. Logue, and R. Sweeney (U.S. Government Printing Office, 1977).

to yield a complete-insulation outcome without employing implausible simplifying assumptions directly responsible for that result.[22]

European and North American policymakers in real life experience the same dilemma highlighted in this illustration. The financial and real-sector interdependencies between Europe and North America are much too pervasive to be neutralized by any degree or form of variability in the exchange relations between the EEC currencies and the dollar.

There is an element of truth in the conventional wisdom about the insulating properties of flexible exchange rates. The consequences for a nation's economy of policy actions and nonpolicy disturbances originating abroad do vary in magnitude under different external monetary policies. For most if not all domestic macroeconomic policy actions taken abroad and for many types of nonpolicy disturbances, the effects spill over *less* into the home country if the national currency is permitted to appreciate in response to external stimuli that are expansionary and to depreciate in response to those that are contractionary. Again, however, this element of truth does not constitute an unqualified recommendation in favor of more rather than less exchange-rate variability. The partial insulation of rate variability must be seen in the light of two further, equally important points.

First, the buffering tendencies associated with variability do *not* apply to every type of disturbance originating abroad. Recall, for example, the illustrative disturbance in which private investors in Europa reduced their demand for ecu money and increased their demand for ecu-denominated securities. That internal disturbance in Europa adversely influenced economic activity in America when the exchange rate was permitted to adjust, but did not have disruptive effects on American activity when the exchange rate was held unchanged. Thus, in instances such as financial-market disturbances abroad, national policymakers may be *least* effective in buffering the effects of the disturbance if they refrain from exchange-market intervention and permit the exchange rate to float.

Second, the buffering tendencies associated with exchange-rate variability are not always beneficial. Policymakers should not want their nation to be insulated from the rest of the world in periods dominated

22. The conventional wisdom of the insulation position evolved when theoretical analysis of international macroeconomics tended to ignore *financial* interdependence. Models that focus exclusively on the current account in the balance of payments and the direct interdependence of real sectors (implicitly or explicitly assuming an absence of all international capital flows except changes in official reserve assets) can yield the complete-insulation outcome.

by disturbances originating within the real sector of their own economy. And if a nation's policymakers take policy actions that turn out to have been mistakes, they will be less unhappy in retrospect if the consequences of their mistakes spill over into the rest of the world to the greatest possible extent.

In a nirvana designed explicitly for them, nationally myopic policymakers would be able simultaneously to retain within their home economy the benefits of good things originating at home, to export as much as possible of their own nation's bad things to the rest of the world, to import good things from the rest of the world, and to insulate the home economy from all bad things originating in the rest of the world. Mere allusion to that nirvana, however, exposes its illusory nature. Any dream of achieving that nirvana by means of some once-and-for-all decision about the form and degree of exchange-rate variability is a still more forlorn hope.

Implications for International Cooperation

The discussion until this point has emphasized the perspective of policymakers in a single nation or a group of nations such as the European Economic Community. That myopic outlook needs to be corrected with a systemic analysis of the world economy as a whole. For under the conditions of intermediate interdependence, individual nations or regional groups of nations cannot successfully pursue independent macroeconomic policies.

The constraints on a nation's freedom to take independent policy actions manifest themselves most obviously in the choice of an external monetary policy. In the analytical world of Europa and America, there are two central banks but only one exchange rate. Just as the two central banks in that world cannot act independently to set the single exchange rate at two different exogenous levels, N central banks in the actual world economy cannot act independently to set $N - 1$ exchange rates at N exogenous levels. Apart from increases in the world total stock, one nation cannot acquire (spend) outside reserve assets without another nation simultaneously using (receiving) them. Nor can one nation accumulate or run down external reserve assets in currency-denominated form without generating counterpart changes in external reserve liabilities for another country.

Because all nations cannot successfully implement external monetary policies of their own independent choosing, some minimum degree of consultation and cooperation about exchange rates and external reserve positions is inevitable. When a common world policy exists as the result of prior agreement among nations about their individual external policies, as in the postwar Bretton Woods regime, the resulting exchange-rate and external-reserves arrangements are typically labeled "the international monetary system." When such agreement is lacking or partially lacking, as in the period since March 1973, the de facto outcome for the world is a happenstance—an "international monetary non-system" resulting from the interplay of inconsistent national policies.[23]

The fourth view identified at the outset of this paper, that nations should agree on some new supranational rule of law for exchange rates and external reserves, derives its force from recognition of the inevitable non-independence of nations' external monetary policies and from a dislike of the possible consequences of anarchy.

The difficulty with the international monetary reform position is that it fails to pursue the logic of its own argument far enough. The non-independence of national policy actions extends well beyond external monetary policies. As suggested earlier, an internally consistent analysis of a world economy characterized by intermediate interdependence shows that the effectiveness of a nation's domestic policies depends not only on the expenditure and asset decisions of its own residents and not only on the international monetary system, but also on the domestic policies and private-sector domestic decisions of foreign nations. Any extra room for maneuver in one nation's domestic policies associated with the openness of its economy necessarily comes at the expense of domestic policy flexibility for other nations.

Given the non-independence of nations' domestic as well as external policies, restriction of international cooperation to the area of exchange rates and external reserve positions is bound to be analytically unsound. The difficulties can be especially great if an attempt is made to impose a tightly drafted supranational rule of law pertaining exclusively to the international monetary system.

The simplest laws that can be uniformly applied to all nations are rules of thumb with provisions for exceptions only in extreme circumstances. The two leading candidates on grounds of simplicity are: "do not

23. Even in a non-system, a substantial amount of consultation takes place about exchange-market intervention to avoid noncooperative actions that are flatly at cross purposes.

change the exchange rate except in case of fundamental disequilibrium" and "do not dirty the float unless the exchange market becomes very disorderly." But these rules of thumb are merely a lawyer's version of the minimum-variance and untrammeled-market positions, each of which is markedly inferior, some of the time, for all nations.

A looser formulation of supranational law that deals exclusively with exchange rates and external reserves, while less problematic than inflexible rules of thumb, is still subject to the same fundamental difficulty. From the perspective of individual nations or regional groups of nations, there is no logically valid dividing line between "external" and "domestic" policy decisions. Nor can the external and domestic sectors of a national or regional economy be validly analyzed in isolation. If supranational traffic regulations were written to conform to the realities of non-independence, their scope would have to be extended to the entire range of domestic as well as external macroeconomic policies.[24]

Should national governments be urged to develop such a comprehensive rule of law for the world economy and to subject their domestic policy actions to corresponding enforcement responsibilities of supranational institutions? A sufficient reason for rejecting that recommendation is its obvious impracticality. Despite the economic interdependence that undermines their sovereignty de facto, national governments are politically unable to take major steps to cede a substantial part of their sovereignty de jure.

Even if domestic politics would permit national governments to yield some sovereignty, an effort to write a comprehensive rule of law for the world economy could not deal with the most important problems caused by macroeconomic non-independence. One must have a naive view of the role of law to accept the notion that nations can first agree on a covenant articulating rules for acceptable behavior (and proscribing certain types of behavior as unacceptable), and can thereafter make independent decisions within that legal environment without creating serious problems for each other. Laws do not (and cannot) play such an efficacious role in regulating the behavior of individuals within a national

24. The amended Articles of Agreement of the International Monetary Fund (in force since April 1978) mention general obligations to promote financial and economic stability (such as in Article I), but the operational emphasis (as in Article IV) is on the exchange-rate policies of member countries. With the exception of a caveat and one important reference that gets the camel's nose into the tent, the IMF guidelines for the "Surveillance over Exchange Rate Policies" (adopted in May 1977) do not even mention domestic macroeconomic policies; see International Monetary Fund, *IMF Survey* (April 3, 1978), p. 107.

society. Nor does a well-functioning legal system for the domestic society obviate the need for positive collective action to supply "public goods."[25] Cooperative decisionmaking about national macroeconomic policies is a prime example of an international public good. Its promotion requires discretionary collective action by national governments, not development of a supranational rule of law.[26]

In sum, it is not possible to devise a supranational rule of law for the regulation of macroeconomic interactions of national economies that would be both politically feasible and analytically sound. If interdependence among national economies continues to grow as it has in the last three decades, moreover, it will be increasingly inappropriate to concentrate any "reform" efforts on the international monetary system alone.

Where does this conclusion leave international cooperation? From a systemic perspective, what can be done to promote as healthy and stable an evolution of the world economy as possible? National governments in Europe and North America, and in the world as a whole, have three broad choices in collectively managing their economic interrelations.

The first choice is to try to find low-cost and mutually acceptable ways to "dis-integrate" the world economy, or at least to inhibit any further integration. Impediments to movements of goods, assets, and people across national boundaries reduce benefits for some individuals. But they may permit somewhat more autonomy for national macroeconomic policies and, for good or for ill, may to a greater extent bottle up the consequences of policy actions and nonpolicy disturbances in the nation in which they originate. If nations place a very high value on being able to experience divergent macroeconomic outcomes, efforts should be made to devise ingenious impediments to international transactions that yield a large gain in autonomy for as small a sacrifice as possible of the benefits of interdependence.[27]

25. See, for example, Mancur Olson, *The Logic of Collective Action: Public Goods and the Theory of Groups,* 2d ed. (Harvard University Press, 1971).

26. For discussion of this point and a more extensive presentation of the argument in this section, see chapter 25 of my *Money and Monetary Policy*.

27. See, for example, James Tobin's suggestion for an internationally uniform tax on spot exchange transactions designed to produce a greater segmentation of financial markets for assets denominated in different currencies. Tobin first made the proposal in *The New Economics, One Decade Older* (Princeton University Press, 1974), pp. 88–92, and recently elaborated it in "A Proposal for International Monetary Reform," presidential address to the 1978 annual meeting of the Eastern Economic Association, Discussion Paper 506 (Cowles Foundation for Research in Economics, Yale University, 1978).

The second possible course for national governments is to maintain governmental institutions and decisionmaking behavior in essentially their present form. Domestic macroeconomic policies, for example, would be made, as now, with only minimal international consultation; international monetary arrangements would permit national discretion in the choice of external monetary policy. Even if the underlying degree of economic interdependence continues to increase, governments would try to avoid new protectionist and regulatory measures that impede transactions across national boundaries. This would be a passive but not necessarily irresponsible posture.

The third course is to try to find mutually acceptable ways to increase cooperative decisionmaking about national macroeconomic policies and thereby to improve the performance of the world economy. This course would not only accept increasing interdependence, but would actively try to promote a corresponding evolution of national and supranational institutions to deal with it.

A discussion of the arguments for and against these broad choices falls outside the scope of this paper. I merely note here my own tentative conclusions. The passive course, I believe, is likely to get ruled out on political grounds as time goes on. Controlled dis-integration, no matter how ingenious, is likely to prove either impossible or excessively costly. Difficult though it will be, therefore, I believe the best course is to try actively to adapt to increasing interdependence, and thereby to manage it better. Among other things, that course implies learning the lessons of collective action internationally that have been learned (or in some cases are still being learned) within individual nations.

Whichever of the three courses one thinks should characterize economic interrelations between Europe and North America in the 1980s, it should at least be clear that international cooperation should not be preoccupied with the form and degree of exchange-rate variability per se. The awkward fact is that Europe and North America are sometimes better off when exchange rates are allowed to move and at other times better off when they are not. A second awkward fact is that the behavior of exchange rates preferable for Europe may at times be undesirable for North America, and vice versa. The most important economic issues faced by Europe and North America, however, stem from the many financial and real-sector interdependencies that link them together; these determine the course of the world economy whatever happens to exchange rates. The more that policymakers and analysts allow themselves to be distracted by the artificial debate between the minimum-variance and the untrammeled-market positions or by narrowly conceived efforts to reform the international monetary system, the less progress they can make in coming to practical grips with the problems of interdependence.

APPENDIX

Charts of Exchange-Rate Variability, 1970-80, for Germany, France, Italy, the United Kingdom, Japan, Canada, and the United States

To facilitate comparison, all series are index numbers with the same base (March 1973 = 100) plotted over the same time period (January 1970 to April 1980), and the vertical scales on the charts have identical intervals. Data are from the Federal Reserve Board and the Morgan Guaranty Trust Company of New York.

Germany: Alternative Measures of the External Value of the Mark, 1970–80

Monthly averages of daily exchange rates (March 1973 = 100)

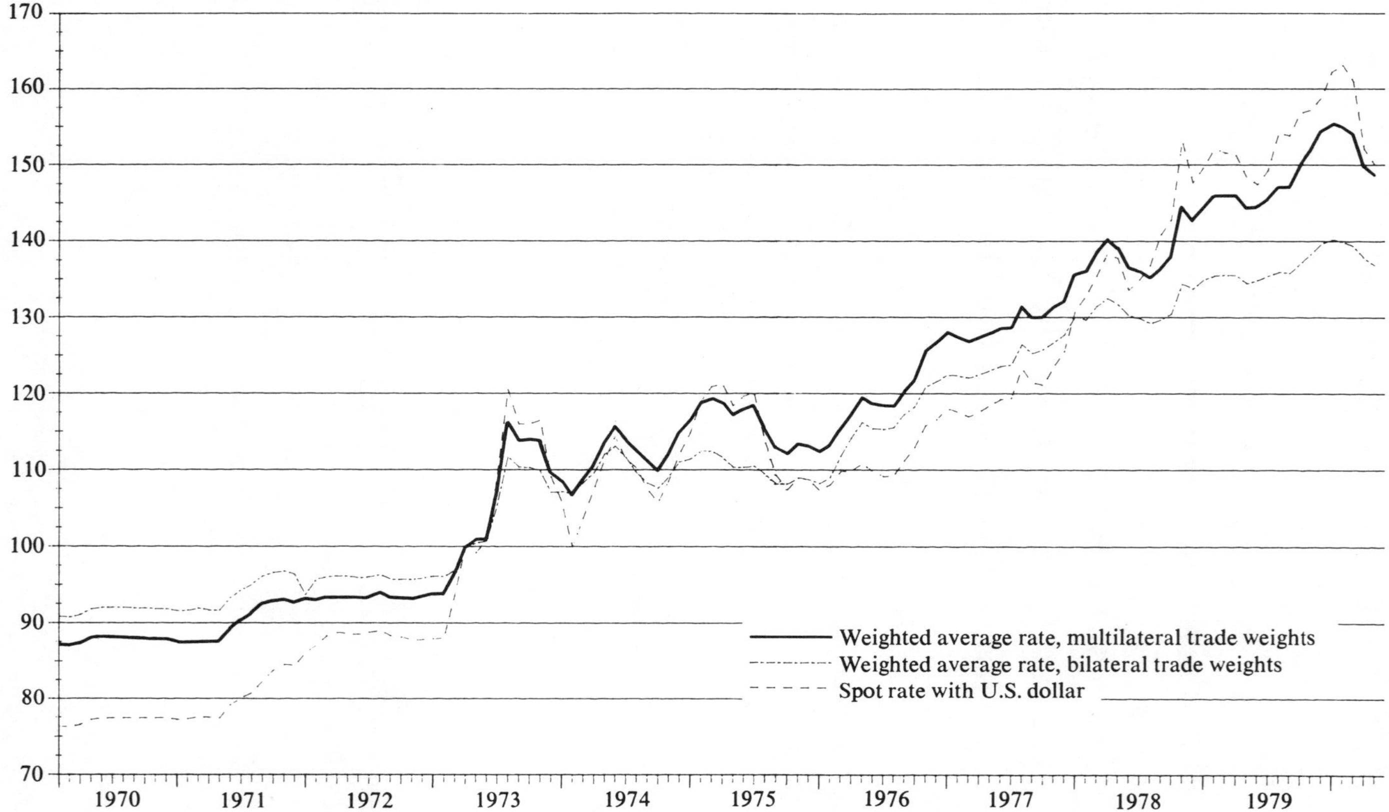

France: Alternative Measures of the External Value of the Franc, 1970–80

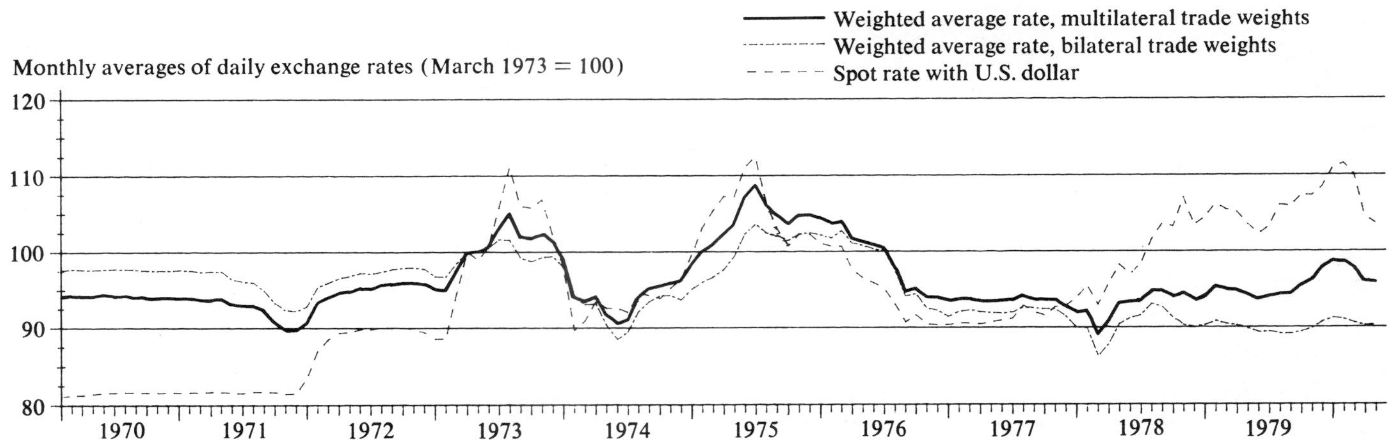

Italy: Alternative Measures of the External Value of the Lira, 1970–80

Monthly averages of daily exchange rates (March 1973 = 100)

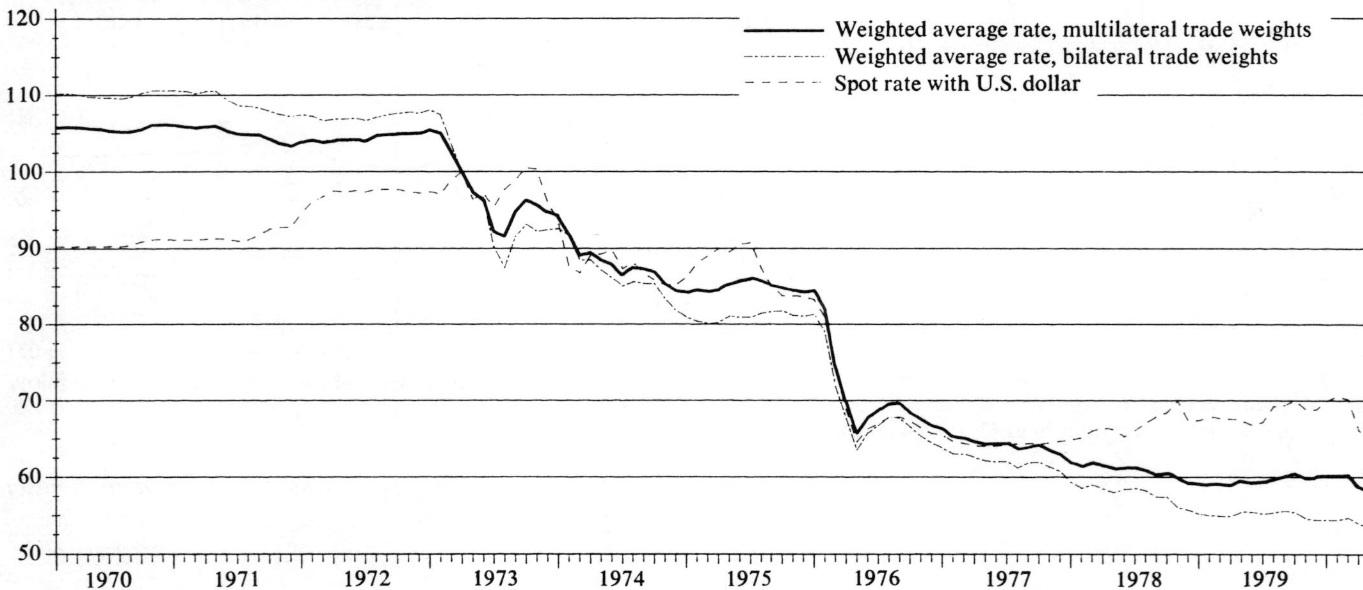

United Kingdom: Alternative Measures of the External Value of the Pound Sterling, 1970–80

Monthly averages of daily exchange rates (March 1973 = 100)

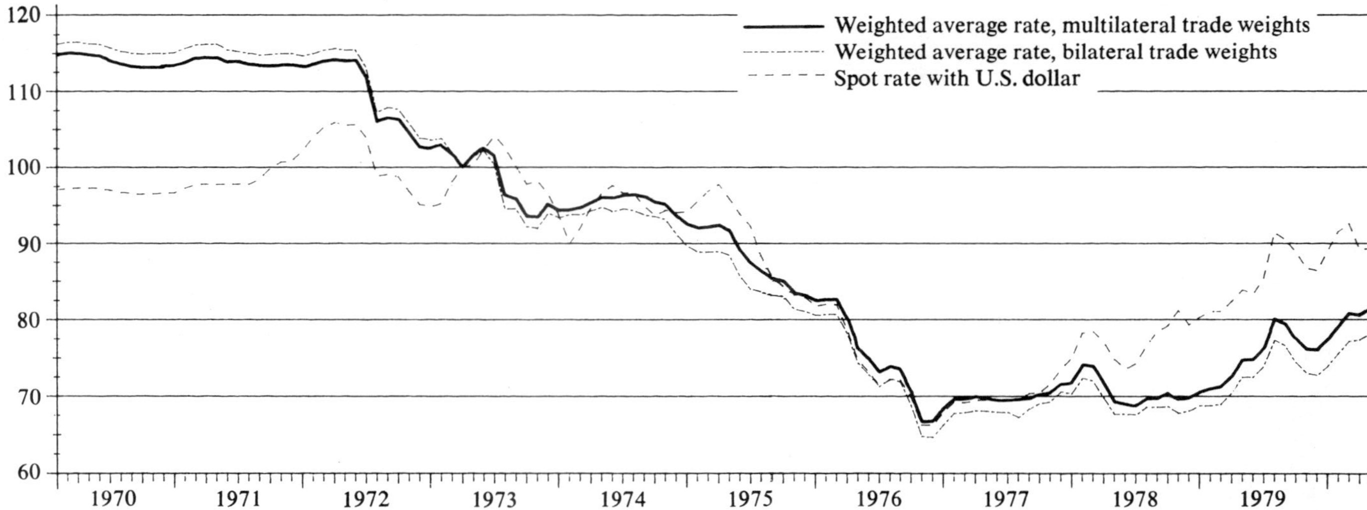

Japan: Alternative Measures of the External Value of the Yen, 1970–80

Monthly averages of daily exchange rates (March 1973 = 100)

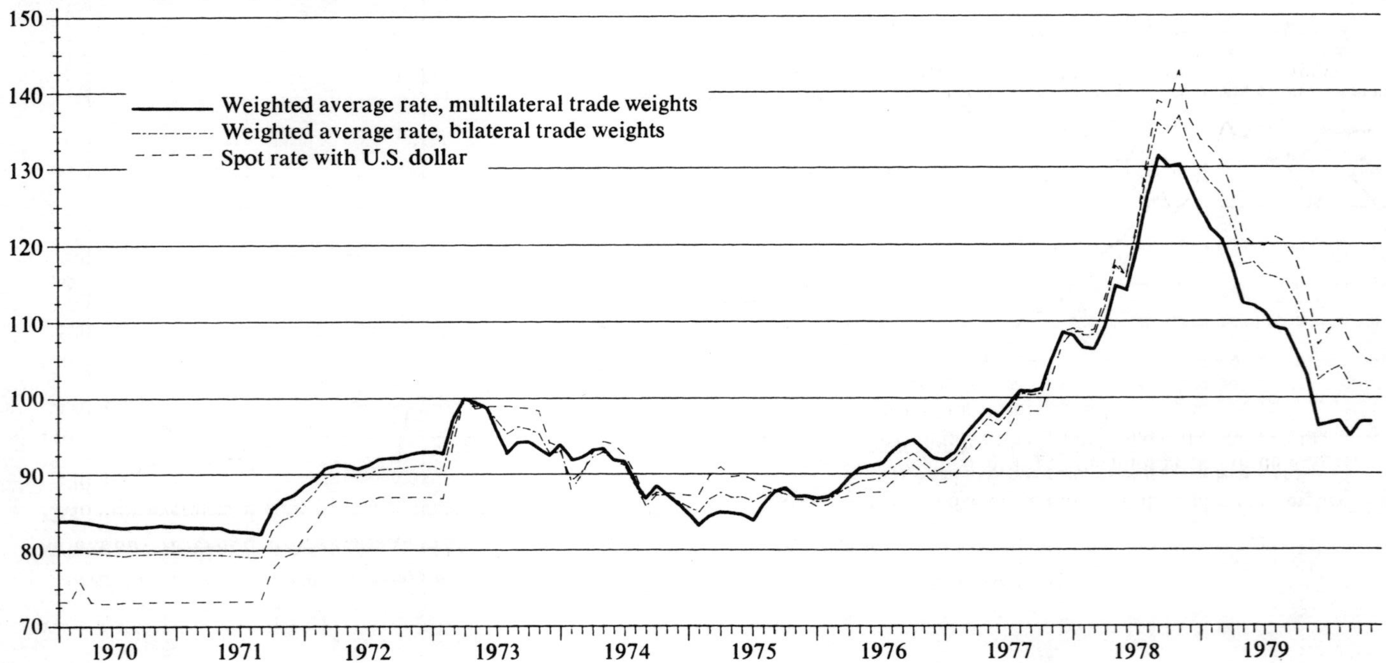

Canada: Alternative Measures of the External Value of the Canadian Dollar, 1970–80

Monthly averages of daily exchange rates (March 1973 = 100)

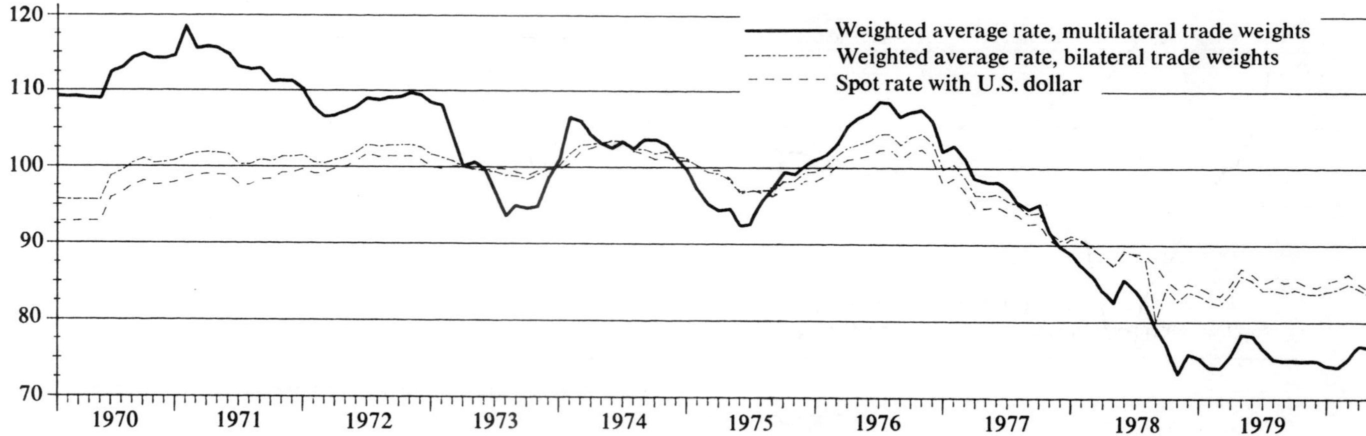

United States: Alternative Measures of the External Value of the U.S. Dollar, 1970–80

Monthly averages of daily exchange rates (March 1973 = 100)

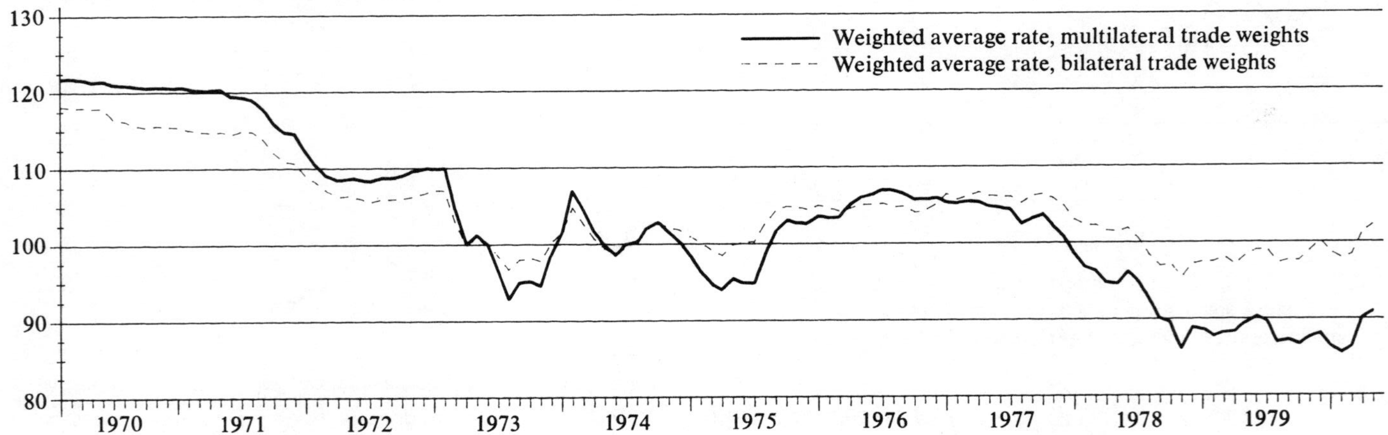